MW00897330

Rooted in Christ

72 Days of Growing in Your Identity in Christ

- Devotional & Journal -

Additional programs and resources by Fit+Faith include:

The Rooted in Christ Podcast

The Healthy Christian Women Podcast

7 Day Detox Checklist

7 Day Meal Plan Bundle

Slim Down Support Kit

Health Trilogy Toolkit

BeautifulYOU™

Heart-First Health™

Identity Declaration Guide

Rooted in Christ

72 Days of Growing in Your Identity in Christ

- Devotional & Journal -

Dr. Melody Stevens

FIT+FAITH

Fit+Faith Publishing
2020

First Printing: 2020

ISBN 978-1-79489-674-1

Fit+Faith Publishing
P.O. Box 370917
San Diego, CA 92137

www.fitplusfaith.com

Ordering Information:

Special discounts are available on quantity purchases by corporations, associations, educators, and others. For details, contact the publisher at the above listed address.

U.S. trade bookstores and wholesalers: Please contact Fit+Faith.

Tel: (619) 537-9941 or email support@fitplusfaith.com

Dedication

This Book and all other publications and resources from Fit+Faith are dedicated first and foremost to our loving Creator, who is The One Who Makes All Things New. Thank you, Jesus, for never giving up on me and gently leading me on the paths of righteousness. Without you, I am nothing.

I also dedicate this book to my sweetheart and loving husband, Matt. No one has loved me more, stood by me, encouraged my dreams and held me in higher esteem than I could ever be worthy of. Your love for me is a tangible reflection of God's love. Thank you for your unwavering belief in me. Who knew that at 15 we would begin our lifelong journey together. God knew. And I'm ever so grateful.

Contents

Acknowledgements

I wish to acknowledge the Ladies of the Fit+Faith community.

Each and every one of you have helped shape this ministry and been a vital part of others' healing. You are the truest example of the Body of Christ around the world, and I am humbled to serve you and to have crossed paths with you on this side of Heaven.

Thank you to the brave women who have shared their stories within these pages to be a testimony of God's redemption and encouragement to others. I love you all. A special thank you to Julie Gill, Jayme Kissee, Melinda Bush, Mary Wasley, Terrie Bearden and Cynthia Parish.

Preface

I want you to get the most out of this powerful journey, so here's the best way to utilize this devotional and journal:

Grab your Bible. Each day also includes journaling space for you, but you may use a separate journal if you wish. You will get more leverage out of each day if you write your thoughts and your declarations out. It doesn't matter to me how you journal, it's just important that you do it.

If you want an accelerated experience, begin our free **14-Day Identity in Christ Challenge**. It condenses these 72 days into a powerful 14-day experience. We also have an incredible global Facebook community to support you along the way. Register for free at https://bit.ly/identitychallenge

How to use this devotional:

1. Each day you will have Bible verses to look up and read. Pray, meditate and study these.

2. You will then read a thought-provoking reflection and will journal your reflections and inspirations with the given prompts.

3. Lastly, you will speak life and truth over yourself by reading the daily identity declaration, *out loud,* adding your name in it.

In this way you will use your voice to declare life and victory over yourself, thus powerfully renewing your mind in Christ.

Get ready for an incredible ride of diving deeper into who God created you to be. Live in the divine power of your Identity in Christ.

~Dr. Melody

Introduction

It was the summer of 2015 and I was treating my patients in my physical therapy clinic, when I could no longer ignore the call. God had begun speaking to my heart, and as much as I wanted to listen and obey, I was scared because it was going to disrupt everything.

How could I up and leave the practice I had built? What God had called me to build. Why would He be changing things when we were just getting started and just getting settled? But the longer I ignored the tugging in my heart, the stronger it became.

"Fine, God. I'll do something about it."

And the Fit+Faith blog was born. An outlet to provide encouragement, resources and discussion around how our spiritual life directly plays into every other facet of our lives. "Are you satisfied now?" I asked.

And truth be told, I really liked this message in my heart, and getting the word out, but how could I abandon everything I had done up until that point? I thought I had placated the voice in my head by starting the blog, but the longer it went on, the more it spread, pretty soon I was consumed and it was all I could think about.

This was my true calling!

God knew what He was doing all along. But change is hard. And I had mixed feelings and wrestled with fully committing for a few years. I'm ever so grateful for God's love and patience, aren't you?

God knew it wasn't easy, but often the best things are made even more precious in the pursuit.

Fast forward five years, and Fit+Faith has grown into an international community of Christian women, all on a mission to honor and serve the Lord with a healthy mind, body and spirit. And now God has taken us on another turn.

This devotional was birthed from an outlet to nurture our spiritual health, and we first created a 14-Day Identity in Christ Challenge.

The Challenge was so powerful, and the Holy Spirit was working so tangibly in women's lives, that God inspired me to expand the content and verses from the Challenge into what you now hold in your hands.

First we created a gorgeous digital pdf ebook version, and now we've translated it into a paperback. There's nothing quite like holding and reading a tangible book, am I right?

And the final surprise that has sprung up from all of this is we now also have an accompanying Rooted in Christ Podcast for those who prefer auditory content. It's been an incredible ride.

What you're about embark upon holds the power to change your life. Your outlook, your motives, your healing, your effectiveness for God's Kingdom.

And it's not from anything that I might say or write per-say, but from the power of God's Word and you opening yourself to the healing and redemption that Jesus offers you.

Take this journey seriously. Give God your next 72 days and experience all He has in store. You will not regret even a single day. Open your Bible, grab your journal, and set your heart to hear from God and allow Him to transform every area of your life.

He has only the best in store for you, even though the journey is often not what we expect. We can trust our unknown future to a known God. Growing in your identity in Christ is the most worthwhile thing you will ever do.

Let's begin.

Your Identity in Christ

Days 1 to 72

DAY 1

Meditate on the Living Word...
- Romans 8:28-39

Reflect:

I love these verses in Romans 8. One of the most powerful chapters in all the Bible. Who or what can separate us from the love of God? Nothing and no one. In Him we are more than conquerors over anything that attempts to separate us from the love of God. There is no place that God's love cannot go. No depth too low or place too far that His love cannot reach. If we ever needed reason to praise Him, there is not greater than this.

Journal:
- What does it mean to you to be more than a conqueror?
- What are some circumstances that feel insurmountable right now?
- How would you approach them differently when you're living in your identity as more than a Conqueror?

DECLARE:

I, _____, am more than a Conqueror through Him who loves me.

JOURNAL

DAY 2

Meditate on the Living Word...

- Revelation 12:10-12

Reflect:

So often we can feel like our torment in this life will never end. Like the enemy has a foothold and we can never shake him, let alone crush him. But stand firm. Be steadfast! Although it may seem dark at times, your victory in this life is assured because of the power of Jesus. Use your story, your testimony, to defeat the evil one, claiming victory in Jesus' name.

Journal:

- Write out today's declaration and reflect on how your identity as an Overcomer in Christ changes your view and perspective of trials and temporary struggles.
- What trials are you facing right now that need this truth and new perspective? All things in this life are temporary, even when they seem unending, but our true home is in eternity with Christ.

DECLARE:

I, _____, am an Overcomer by the blood of the Lamb and the word of my testimony.

*Don't miss reading Cynthia's testimony on page 6...

JOURNAL

CYNTHIA'S STORY (DAY 2)

My story is especially difficult and messy, and I made every possible mistake, but because of God's plan, I survived.

I was adopted at four weeks old to a loving family but as time went by things changed. I was sexually abused by a neighbor when I was 5 and at the age of 7 it started with my brother. After telling my secret to my mother, instead of being protected and defended, I heard, "whore, disgraceful slut" and thus began a lifelong battle with shame. I was bounced around between my mother's house and my Aunt and by 7th grade I started being promiscuous with boys. In 9th grade I began drinking, doing drugs and running away. By the age of 14 I was given over to the state and was running away from foster homes and group homes. Looking for love and acceptance in all the wrong places, I wound up as a teenage prostitute before my 17th birthday. Within a year I was pregnant and desperate and had a late-term abortion alone in a hotel room. Soon thereafter I testified against my pimp in front of a grand jury and never heard from him again.

At 18 I got a job, got pregnant again, and Randy and I were married shortly after I emancipated. The memory of my mother's disapproving glares and vicious comments on my wedding day are the last memory I have of her. I was married in April, by May she was in the hospital, unable to communicate. She died in June.

Soon the controlling and manipulative nature of my husband came out. I just wanted to be safe, but I knew I couldn't stay. I took out a student loan and I ran again, this time with 3 young children in tow, still looking for a place to belong. I celebrated my 30th birthday as finally being old enough to be divorced with 3 kids.

A few years later I had married again and had another daughter but soon my husband began bringing pornography into our home. I had everything I thought I needed to be happy and still I lost it. I must be doing something wrong. The worthless, discarded, shameful girl of my past came back with a vengeance. I called the suicide helpline on my scariest day, afraid I'd hurt myself or Sophie. And that gave me enough relief from my anxiety to begin to sort through the things I needed to survive. I moved into my own apartment and began seeing a counselor. God started using strategic people at work to begin showing me His true love and He began moving in my heart again.

I showed up for a service on a hot August Sunday, sat alone in a pew and spoke to no one on my way in. But as soon as I began to squeak out a song, a praise, a worship, I felt the Holy Spirit surround me. In tears I heard his comforting words of reassurance. "You are safe, you are loved, you are home."

I praise the Lord that didn't allow me to become an abuser when I was abused. I praise the Lord that didn't allow me to become violent when I was assaulted. I praise the Lord that didn't allow me to become bitter when everything failed.

I praise the Lord that didn't allow me to become angry when I was attacked. I Praise the Lord that protected my kindness and compassion when my world was harsh and unfeeling.

I praise the Lord that carried me away from death when I put myself in harm's way.

I praise the Lord that sacrificed his Son so that I may live.

Meditate on the Living Word...

- 2 Peter 1:3-4

Reflect:

What a power-packed notion to contemplate. The fact that through His power and knowledge, WE are able to participate in His divine nature. And that He has given us promises that we can firmly set our life upon. How gracious is God, who doesn't need us, but chooses to love us and share His divinity with us. May our praise be never-ending for who He is, what He's done for us, and what He gives us access to.

Journal:

- What does it mean to you to be a partaker of the Divine?
- Express your praise and your longing to grow in knowledge and wisdom, so you may take hold of that which Christ took hold of you.

DECLARE:

I, _____, am a partaker of His divine nature.

JOURNAL

Meditate on the Living Word...

- 2 Corinthians 5:16-21

Reflect:

When you are an Ambassador, you carry the full legal and political authority of whatever or whomever you represent. God is asking us to take our Ambassadorship seriously, as He already sacrificed His son so we would be able to be reconciled with him. The price has already been paid. It's time to step into your legal authority in Christ and represent Him well.

Journal:

- What does it mean to you to be an Ambassador for Christ? What does it look like, what does it entail?
- Ask the Lord for guidance on what actions He wants you to take, as His ambassador. How does being His Ambassador change how you normally conduct yourself?
- Where are you not living up to your true title, and where are you not taking advantage of all that is yours to partake?

DECLARE:

I, _____, am an ambassador for Christ.

JOURNAL

"Give thanks in all circumstances; for this is God's will for you in Christ Jesus."

I THESSALONIANS 5:18

Meditate on the Living Word...
- 1 Peter 2:4-10

Reflect:

Think of the implication of being specifically chosen by God. So often we don't feel worthy of being chosen. We know our misdeeds, we know our sins, and we feel unworthy of God's love, acceptance and forgiveness. But God, seeing all of these things, nothing being hidden from Him, still saw so much value in us that He created the path for our restoration to Him through Jesus Christ. God has chosen you.

Journal:

Write your declaration and write your praise and thanksgiving to God who chose you, in spite of yourself. In spite of your sin. He still knows and loves you. Praise Him for His goodness.

DECLARE:

I, _____, am part of a chosen generation, a royal priesthood, a holy nation, a purchased people.

JOURNAL

DAY 6

Meditate on the Living Word...

- 2 Corinthians 5:21

Reflect:

What love. That He who knew no sin, became sin for us, that we might become the righteousness of God. God wants you to partake in His righteousness. To experience it NOW, not waiting until you get to Heaven. And we must understand that we cannot become righteousness by our own work or merit. It is in Christ alone that we become God's righteousness. Without Christ we are nothing.

Journal:

Where have you found yourself trying to become righteous on your own? Of your own merit, your own accord?

Repent right now, and ask God to change your heart, that you may fully understand that without Christ you can never be worthy or righteous in your own strength. Praise Him that Jesus makes a way!

DECLARE:

I, _____, am the righteousness of God in Jesus Christ.

JOURNAL

Meditate on the Living Word...
- 1 Corinthians 6:18-20

Reflect:

God makes it quite plain that we are to honor Him through how we treat, use and care for our bodies. We are not to be involved in sexual immorality and we are not to mistreat what is now a Holy Temple. Once you have accepted Christ and the Holy Spirit in your life, your body is an active temple. We must cherish and care for it accordingly.

Journal:
- Reflect on the ways you may have mistreated your body. Or possibly others have mistreated it/you. Spend time in prayer seeking the Lord for forgiveness both for others and for yourself.
- Cry out to Him and in sincere repentance vow to view and treat your body as the Holy Temple it has been bought as. Jesus paid for you. Let's honor that sacrifice.

DECLARE:

I, _____, am the temple of the Holy Spirit,
I am not my own.

* Don't miss reading Julie's testimony on page 20...

JOURNAL

JULIE'S STORY (DAY 7)

All my life, I have struggled with my weight, many ups on the scale and many downs. As I meditated on these words, I realized, I had a head knowledge but not a heart knowledge. Holy Spirit tugged on my heart to spend time consistently in reviewing and writing out these words.

I began to realize in my health journey, I had included God in everything else in my life, but not in taking care of my health. I started to invite God into this part of my life, seeking His Wisdom. God has changed this part of me, working from the inside out. I realized I had to get to the roots of my health journey in not being able to maintain a healthy weight.

It really has not been about the numbers on the scale but praying for Holy Spirit wisdom as I go throughout each day. God has healed the emptiness of what I was allowing food to fill, yet still feeling hungry. I am now satisfied because God is healing the empty places and wounds. I understand now within my heart what it means to be filled with God's Joy and honor His Holy Temple.

*Make new friends and join our global community on Facebook. Search '**Healthy Christian Women**' and join us.*

"I have been crucified with Christ and I no longer live, but Christ lives in me. The life I now live in the body, I live by faith in the Son of God, who loved me and gave himself for me."

GALATIANS 2:20

DAY 8

Meditate on the Living Word...
- Deuteronomy 28:9-14

Reflect:

Bountiful blessings come from obeying the Lord and heeding His commands. Although this passage is in the Old Testament, it still rings true for us. God blesses His people and honors their obedience. We reap consequences both for obedience and disobedience...let us be wise and heed His word.

Journal:

- What does it mean to you to be the head and not the tail? Above and not beneath? Where might you be living as though this were not true? Where have you been living and acting as though you were the tail and you were beneath?

- Seek repentance before the Lord today, and ask Him for strength and guidance to begin taking your rightful place as His daughter.

DECLARE:

I, _____, am the head and not the tail; I am above only and not beneath.

JOURNAL

Meditate on the Living Word...
- Matthew 5:14-16

Reflect:

Think about being a light. Others need it for vision. For guidance. For warmth. For direction. If the light were gone, they would be lost. They would fail and flounder. God is telling that we were meant to be lights! What kind of light are you giving off? Dim, dull? Or bright, clear, shining? Others are looking to you and depending upon your light, and God will use you to be a blessing to them. Don't hide your light.

Journal:

- Reflect on the quality of your spiritual light. Where and how is it being dulled? Where do you need to grow in confidence, knowledge, wisdom for your light to shine brighter?
- Reflect on what lies you may be trapped in that are dulling your light. Speak out against them in the power of Jesus' name. You were meant to shine! And the only way to shine the brightest is to make way for God to shine for you. It is not your burden or responsibility. You are only to be a transparent vessel for the light of God to shine through you.

DECLARE:

I, _____, am the light of the world.

JOURNAL

DAY 10

Meditate on the Living Word...

- Romans 8:31-33
- Colossians 3:12-15

Reflect:

Wow. Think of the honor of being God's elect. As His elect we are to act and conduct ourselves in a certain way. Not pompous, arrogant or self-righteous. But kind, tender, generous, humble, long-suffering: Like Jesus.

Journal:

- How to the expectations of how God's elect are to act, match up to your typical daily life? Are you displaying these qualities as your default? If not, confess and repent right now.
- Ask God to move and change your heart so that you are taken over my His divine nature, and removing the sinful man from inside more and more.
- Ask Him to reveal where your shortcomings are originating, and ask for His guidance and healing.

DECLARE:

I, _____, I am His elect, full of mercy, kindness, humility, and long suffering.

JOURNAL

Meditate on the Living Word...

- Ephesians 1:7-12

Reflect:

Is there any greater blessing than being forgiven? When we sincerely ask, we are not only forgiven of our "small" sins, but of ALL of our sins. All sin is equal in God's eyes. Take a moment to have a praise party that you are forgiven of ALL trespasses against a holy God. We don't deserve it, yet He loves us so much that He has done it. Thank you, Jesus, that through your innocent blood, we are cleansed.

Journal:

- Reflect on what you've been forgiven of. Reflect on the sacrifice it took for Jesus to pay that penalty for you.

- Reflect on who you need to forgive, as you were first forgiven (and this includes forgiving yourself.)

- Forgiveness is a priceless and powerful gift, meant for receiving, and for giving to others. Do not be stingy. Forgive quickly and fully. Christ has already done the same for you. Who are you to hold back on someone else? Ask Christ for strength, and let it go.

DECLARE:

I, _____, am forgiven of all my sins and washed in the Blood.

JOURNAL

Meditate on the Living Word...

▪ Colossians 1:12-14

Reflect:

God has given us redemption by the blood of Jesus, forgiving our sins and delivered us from the kingdom of darkness. Who else can do that for us? We owe Him everything! It is in Jesus name that we no longer have to live powerless to sin or destruction from the enemy. Jesus' name sets us free! Call on His name today and receive your free gift of deliverance from the evil one. Amen!

Journal:

▪ Reflect and recount all that you can remember that you've been delivered from in Jesus' name. Ask the Holy Spirit for fresh eyes and perspective of the magnitude of what Jesus has done for you. Both in the past, present, and things to come. Let your heart abound with praise!

▪ Ask Him to reveal where your shortcomings are originating, and ask for His guidance and healing.

DECLARE:

I, _____, am delivered from the power of darkness and translated into God's kingdom.

JOURNAL

"As you therefore have received Christ Jesus the Lord, so walk in Him, rooted and built up in Him and established in the faith, as you have been taught, abounding in it with thanksgiving."

COLOSSIANS 2:6-7

DAY 13

Meditate on the Living Word...

- Deuteronomy 28:15-68

- Galatians 3:13

Reflect:

Whew! You made it through! That passage in Deuteronomy is tough!! But then we turn to Galatians 3 and see so clearly that Jesus paid the penalty that was rightfully ours, so that we would not have to pay the price that Deuteronomy lays out. Do you need any greater reason to praise Jesus with your whole heart today?!

Journal:

- Write your declaration and ask God to search your heart if there's any part of you that has been living "less than" what Jesus paid for. He paid for you to be free from sin, redeemed, no longer under the curses of sickness and poverty thinking.

- Seek and repent if needed for any places where you have settled for less than what Jesus paid for and set you free from. If the Son has set you free, *You are free indeed!* It's time to step into it, truly believe it, and start walking in it.

DECLARE:

I, _____, am redeemed from the curse of sin, sickness, and poverty.

JOURNAL

Meditate on the Living Word...

■ Colossians 2:4-10

Reflect:

We come to the cornerstone verses of this devotional. Being rooted in our faith. What comes to mind when you think of being rooted? Unwavering. Unchanged or unphased by the storm. Stable and solid in any season. Deep roots grow over time. Be diligent in your growing in the Lord. The deeper your roots grow now, the better you will be able to weather the storms that may come. You were meant to be firmly planted in Christ. But you must be actively growing.

Journal:

■ Reflect on your current roots. Are they deep and strong, or thin and surface level?

■ Ask the Holy Spirit how He wants you to grow and take action to deepen your roots.

DECLARE:

I, _____, am firmly rooted, built up, established in my faith and overflowing with gratitude.

Don't miss reading Terrie's testimony on page 38...

JOURNAL

I didn't even know that my wrist was broken because I had no feeling in my arms. In a heap on the ground I sat and listened as my 19 month old daughter was throwing up from being thrown against a wall while I was holding her. I put my arm up to protect her head and my head hit the wall along with my arm. He threw us across the floor like we were ragdolls.

That was my life as a young wife. I was told I was fat, ugly, and no good, I had no friends, I could only go to and from church, and I was a prisoner in my own home. I really didn't know any better because I was too ashamed to say anything and when I did reach out to a pastor he told me to stay and be the best wife I could be. Sitting on that floor I told God that I did not believe He was real if He made me stay in that marriage.

Fast forward 42 years and I see the hand of a mighty God on me all of my life. I got free of that horrible situation, my children and I running for our lives. God saw me. He is my El Roi, the God Who sees me.

The turning point came when I started reading through my Bible a few years later and saw Psalm 136. Verse 1 says "Give thanks to the Lord, for He is good; For His lovingkindness is everlasting."
The entire chapter repeats "For His lovingkindness is everlasting."
As I read it out loud I knew that He never left me or would ever forsake me.

Then I found Psalm 5:12 , "For it is Thou who dost bless the righteous man, O Lord, Thou dost surround him with favor as with a shield." I was surrounded with God's favor! Even through those tumultuous 6 years God was going to take all of that and turn it to my good for His glory!

Throughout my life I have been able to sit across from young women in that similar situation and tell them that I understand. While looking into their tearful eyes I can show them, for a fact, that there is hope!

Married 41 years to the man of my dreams, those past years are just that....past. God has redeemed the years the locust had eaten.

I know who I am in Christ!

I am a daughter of the King and He will NEVER let me go.

DAY 15

Meditate on the Living Word...

- 2 Timothy 1:8-12
- Psalm 66:8

Reflect:

Every day we have something to sing praise for. Are you looking for it? Do you see it? Ask the Holy Spirit for eyes to see all that He has blessed you with. We are called to give Him praise. Use the power of your voice to declare truth, thanksgiving and praise to the One who has rescued you from eternal death.

Journal:

- How are you using your voice? Are you taking up the high calling to give praise to the Lord for others to hear, or are you speaking negativity, doubt, death over yourself and others?
- Reign in your tongue, making it a powerhouse of blessing and praise, nothing less. Declare your praise today!

DECLARE:

I, _____, am called of God to be the voice of His praise.

JOURNAL

DAY 16

Meditate on the Living Word...

- Isaiah 53:4-6
- 1 Peter 2:21-25

Reflect:

What love. To lay down one's life for another. Thank you Jesus. Who bore all of our shame and paid the full penalty we owed. It is by His stripes we are healed. Nothing less would have sufficed. He willingly went to the cross, His eyes fixed on us, the joy set before Him. What love.

Journal:

- What sins have been paid by Jesus' stripes? Take a moment to reflect on all the Jesus took on for you.
- Thank God that He remembers our sin no more when we sincerely repent. But it is a blessing in disguise that we cannot forget as easily. It keeps us from quickly returning to those old snares. May we stay far away and ask the Lord for strength and to always see the way out.
- Thank the Lord for His mercies and the price He paid. Do not take it for granted that His stripes set you free.

DECLARE:

I, _____, am healed by the stripes of Jesus.

JOURNAL

"But God, who is rich in mercy, because of His great love with which He loved us, even when we were dead in trespasses, made us alive together with Christ (by grace you have been saved), and raised us up together, and made us sit together in the heavenly places in Christ Jesus..."

EPHESIANS 2:4-6

DAY 17

Meditate on the Living Word...

- Ephesians 2:4-7
- Colossians 2:11-15

Reflect:

I love picturing Jesus triumphing over our iniquities and over any power the enemy had over us, as He won the battle for us, once and for all. The power that raised Him from the dead is the same power that will raise us up to meet Him in glory! Thank you, Jesus! Victory is ours because of You!

Journal:

- Take a moment to picture yourself in glory. Sitting next to Jesus, taking in the sights and sounds of Heaven and reigning with Him. Could there be any greater honor?
- Describe your praise, adoration, devotion, and excitement of what is to come when this life passes away. Eternity awaits, Dear One!

DECLARE:

I, _____, am raised up with Christ and seated in heavenly places.

JOURNAL

Meditate on the Living Word...

- Romans 1:7
- Ephesians 2:4
- Colossians 3:12
- 1 Thessalonians 1:4

Reflect:

Ever been chosen last for something? Not fun. But here's the beauty of God: He Chose Us, *first!* We are chosen. Elected. Greatly loved. Nothing can separate us from His love. Allow this truth to wash over you.

Journal:

- Think to a time when you had been rejected. Discounted. Unwanted. What feelings rise up in these instances?
- Now think about God choosing you, before you had a chance to choose Him. He saw you, loved you, knew you and wanted you. Never doubting for a second that you should be second place, or last place.
- What feelings does that elicit when you think of God's favor and delight in choosing you? Give Him praise today.

DECLARE:

I, _____, am greatly loved by God.

JOURNAL

DAY 19

Meditate on the Living Word...

- Colossians 1:9-12

Reflect:

There will come a day where your strength gives out. We were created with limits. Try as we might, we were never created to do everything in our own strength. We were created to lean on God. To ask and rely on His unending supply of strength. In this passage we read we are strengthened with all might for patience and long-suffering with joy. If you've come to the end of your patience, it's time to switch energy sources.

Journal:

- Where have you found yourself relying on your own strength? What have been the outcome or consequences of that?

- Where are you fearful or distrusting of God that is preventing you from asking and relying on Him for strength to endure?

- Repent of your lack of faith and trust, and begin a new day with the Lord.

DECLARE:

I, _____, am strengthened with all might according to His glorious power.

JOURNAL

Meditate on the Living Word...

- James 4:4-10
- Proverbs 3:34

Reflect:

God is a jealous God. He is jealous of us when we turn to the world and to our own plans and schemes without Him. He has blessings He desires to bestow upon us, but how often do we put Him second, third or even last place in our lives? He opposes our pride and desires us to have a humble heart. In Jesus' name, remaining steadfast in God, we can cause the enemy to flee.

Journal:

- Reflect on where you've allowed the enemy to have a stronghold because you have not submitted yourself fully to the Lord.
- Ask the Holy Spirit to speak to your heart, bring awareness to your mind, and when He does, humble yourself and repent.
- Cast pride, ego and self-centered ambition aside. Let God take over all the places you have left open and vulnerable to the evil one.
- Cry out, "Invade my heart, Oh God, renew a right Spirit within me."

DECLARE:

I, _____, am submitted to God, and the devil flees from me because I resist him in the Name of Jesus.

"Create in me a pure heart, O God, and renew a
steadfast spirit within me."

PSALM 51:10

Meditate on the Living Word...

■ Philippians 3:12-16

Reflect:

I love Paul's imagery of forgetting what is behind, and pressing ahead. How often our past can hold us back. Either we think too highly of it, not reaching for anything greater, or we allow past pain and regret to weigh us down. Regardless of what is behind, let's press on for greater and greater things of the Lord each passing day, until He calls us heavenward. Our work is not yet done.

Journal:

■ Where have you allowed yourself to get stuck in the past? Take some time to repent of where you've allowed regret or pride to hold you back from stepping into what is ahead.

■ Ask the Holy Spirit for fresh vision and be listening for that still small voice.

DECLARE:

I, _____, press on toward the goal to win the prize to which God in Christ Jesus is calling me upward.

JOURNAL

DAY 22

Meltdate on the Living Word...

- 2 Timothy 1:7-9

Reflect:

What an incredible identity. That we have NOT been given a spirit of fear, but of power, love and a sound mind. We are not crazy, we are loved. When fear is closing in, we can rest in knowing we are loved, cared for by God. We are not to be afraid or ruled by fear. We are to call on the Name Above All Names, King Jesus, to break the silence and oppression of fear. *Thank you Jesus!*

Journal:

- Where has fear been wearing you down? Keeping you hidden, frozen, buried under lies of a false identity.

- See the situations surrounded by fear, then see with spiritual eyes what your true Identity in Christ can do about it. You are not powerless. You are not a victim. God is with you. He is for you. And He is carrying you when you are too weak to stand.

- Call out the lies of fear and call in the power, love and sound mind you've been given in Christ.

DECLARE:

For God has not given me, _____, a spirit of fear;
but of power, love, and a sound mind.

JOURNAL

Meditate on the Living Word...
- Galatians 2:19-21

Reflect:

Such powerful words. "It is no longer I who live, but Christ lives in me." Are we truly living this way? Understanding that we have been crucified with Christ? Our flesh is now dead. We are no longer under the rule of sin. We have power over it! But we must choose to actively die to it, and live in Christ. Are we seeking to be the hands, feet and voice of Christ to all we meet and to rise above the futility of our sinful nature? Christ is alive *in us!*

Journal:

- When was the last time I was the hands and feet of Jesus to someone else? Is this a normal occurrence, or was it a rare occasion?

- Where do I continue to get sucked into my sinful desires of the flesh and not live in the power of Christ inside me?

DECLARE:

It is not I, _____, who live, but Christ lives in me,
the hope of Glory.

JOURNAL

DAY 24

Meditate on the Living Word...

■ Colossians 2:8-9

Reflect:

We are complete in Him. The word for *complete* here in the Greek implies filled to capacity, filled up, fullness, to abound. We don't need to seek one more thing (or person) to make us whole. In Jesus we have been filled to capacity, lacking nothing. What comfort that is! Rest in knowing the work has already been done. Your job? Receive it, believe it and walk in it.

Journal:

■ Where do you find yourself looking for things or people to fill you up? Where is your emptiness coming from?

■ Seek the Holy Spirit to reveal the truth to you, so that you may repent of your attempts to fill what God has already made full and complete.

■ Ask for a deeper hunger for things of the Lord, and rest in knowing there is nothing more to do.

DECLARE:

I, _____, am complete in Him Who is the Head of all principalities and power.

JOURNAL

"There is therefore now no condemnation to those who are in Christ Jesus, who do not walk according to the flesh, but according to the Spirit. For the law of the Spirit of life in Christ Jesus has made me free from the law of sin and death."

ROMANS 8:1-2

Meditate on the Living Word...
- Ephesians 2:4-7

Reflect:

Wow. Being made alive in Christ. The Greek here refers to a new moral life, being reanimated conjointly with Christ. We were dead in sin, but then given fresh, new animated life in Christ. Not then to be left alone, but never to be separated from. A completely integrated joint-life with Christ. *How amazing is that?*

Journal:
- How do you feel when you think that because you said "Yes" to Christ, that you were created anew. A joint-creation with Christ, given new life, new hope, new future, new present.
- What does that mean to you, and have you been living from that place? If not, now is the time to step into that fresh anointing and say "Yes" to the new life you've been given.
- God is with you every step of the way. You will never be alone again and have been given a new lease on life! *Start living in it!*

DECLARE:

I, _____, am alive with Christ.

JOURNAL

DAY 26

Meditate on the Living Word...

- Romans 8:1-2

Reflect:

To be free! Liberated. Unencumbered. Unhindered. What a beautiful thing. This is what Christ has done for us. Set us free from the law of sin and death, and given us eternal life that we never could have earned on our own. What a gift. Take hold of it with me today.

Journal:

- Are you truly living as though you're fre? What areas do you still feel you're in spiritual bondage?

- Speak the name of Jesus over these areas and take the next step that someone who was truly free would take. Sometimes all we need is that next step. One step at a time.

- What is your next step? Map it out and go do it. Who the Son sets free, is *free indeed!*

DECLARE:

I, _____, am free from the law of sin and death.

JOURNAL

Meditate on the Living Word...

▪ Isaiah 54:11-17

Reflect:

What beautiful protection God is promising for the servants of the Lord. Are you His faithful servant? Those whose righteousness comes from Him alone. Are you working to create your own righteousness, to be right in your own eyes, or to be submitted and faithful to your Creator? God is looking for those who know and respect their proper place in His Kingdom.

Journal:

▪ Ask the Holy Spirit to reveal any areas where you are attempting to create your own righteousness. Where your pride is inhibiting you from fully surrendering, submitting and obeying the commands of God.

▪ What promises of God are you negating because you do not meet the proper qualifications? Humble yourself, repent where needed and return to a humble submission to God, who promises every good thing to those who love Him and honor Him with obedience.

DECLARE:

I, _____, am far from oppression, and fear does not come near me.

JOURNAL

DAY 28

Meditate on the Living Word...
- 1 John 5:18-21

Reflect:

What a reassurance that because of Jesus we are saved from the evil one and given special understanding in the spirit to discern the word of God or the word of the enemy. We must seek the Lord, taking every thought captive, that we will not be fooled or led astray from the truth and power of God's word.

Journal:
- Where do you feel you're being taunted or misguided by the evil one? We are still under his domain while here on earth. But you are not powerless against him.
- Seek the Holy Spirit in growing in your knowledge, power, authority and action against any schemes the enemy may try to be using to veil your eyes from God's truth.

DECLARE:

I, _____, am born of God, and the evil one does not touch me.

JOURNAL

"Praise be to the God and Father of our Lord Jesus Christ, who has blessed us in the heavenly realms with every spiritual blessing in Christ."

EPHESIANS 1:3

Meditate on the Living Word...
- Ephesians 1:3-10
- 1 Peter 1:13-16

Reflect:

We are called to holy living. Not only has Jesus paid the price for our iniquities, we are not to leave it at that. We are to be responsible in how we act, not taking His grace for granted. We are called to be His living examples, His reflections to the world. And that means striving toward holiness and excellence, yet knowing His grace covers our imperfections.

Journal:
- Where have you caught yourself striving for perfection? Feeling that you needed to work and prove yourself to receive redemption, forgiveness and the favor of God?
- Where have you been caught in works-based legalism? You are FREE from perfectionism. Free from proving yourself. Allow yourself to let those unrealistic expectations go and act as though you truly believe He paid the price to cover all of your shortcomings. Where is God calling you to pursue holiness, yet being mindful that that does not mean perfectionism.

DECLARE:

I, _____, am holy and without blame before Him in love.

JOURNAL

Meditate on the Living Word...

- 1 Corinthians 2:11-16

- Philippians 2:5-11

Reflect:

Having the Mind of Christ. What a mystery. What a privilege. What does it mean to have the mind of Christ? To put others first. To love others as you love yourself. To be a servant leader. To look past the external to the heart. To see everyone as rightly loved by God. Our flesh can often get in the way, but ask for godly eyes to see as Christ sees. He is within you!

Journal:

- Reflect on where you have allowed your flesh and emotions to cloud God's true sight. Ask for forgiveness and for new opportunities to see and treat others as God would have you do.

- Ask the Holy Spirit to reveal the deeper wounds or false beliefs that need healing and restoration so your vision may be clear to see and think with the mind of Christ.

DECLARE:

I, _____, have the mind of Christ.

JOURNAL

DAY 31

Meditate on the Living Word...

- Philippians 4:4-9

Reflect:

One of my favorite passages. Where to set our minds. On whatever is right, admirable, lovely, pure, excellent, praiseworthy. What a stark contrast to where our minds typically get stuck. On negativity, shortcomings, imperfections, gossip etc. When we are fully trusting in the Lord, we can let the rest go and receive peace. Isn't that what we're all after anyway? Peace. It is ours, in Christ.

Journal:

- Where do you need more peace today? What situations seem to be robbing you of peace?

- Letting go is often the hardest thing, but almost always required if we are to exchange our worries for God's peace. Ask God for the courage to lay your burdens down, and to not pick them back up. Be bold in taking that step of faith to trust the Lord like never before.

- How will you faith ever grow if it's never tested or given the circumstances to put it to the test? Step into His peace today, exchanging your troubles for His security.

DECLARE:

I, _____, have the peace of God that passes all understanding.

Don't miss reading Melinda's testimony on page 82...

JOURNAL

I have experienced some hard times in my life.

Our first child passed away at 3 months old from SIDS. Joshua's life was short but packed with great memories. The Sunday before, he woke up from his nap crying and while I was rocking him, I remember a soft voice telling me time was short.

I've also had some serious health challenges and one night I was tired from crying myself to sleep so instead of trying to control it all, I gave it all to God.

Let me tell you, I had peace come over me that could only be from God!

I prayed to please let me keep working to support my family. He did and I never missed a day of work through my radiation treatments!

I am now a 3-year breast cancer survivor, praise God!

Grow in your mental, spiritual and physical health with our Health Trilogy Toolkit. Visit MyHealthTrilogy.com

82

"Finally, brothers and sisters, whatever is true, whatever is noble, whatever is right, whatever is pure, whatever is lovely, whatever is admirable—if anything is excellent or praiseworthy—think about such things."

PHILIPPIANS 4:8

Meditate on the Living Word...
- 1 John 4:4-6

Reflect:

For sheep to not be led astray by an imposter, they only obey their shepherd's call. The same is for us. To not be led astray by the enemy or the world, we must know the voice of our Master intimately, so that everything else can be easily detected as false. We must hide His Word in our hearts so we will not be led astray.

Journal:
- Where have you been so busy trying to sort out the lies of the enemy, that you've lost the still small voice of God?
- How can you begin listening and tuning your ear to the words of your Heavenly Father, so that the lies and half-truths of everything else can fall away?

DECLARE:

I, _____, have the Greater One living in me; greater is He Who is in me than he who is in the world.

JOURNAL

DAY 33

Meditate on the Living Word...

■ Romans 5:17-21

Reflect:

This is great news! I love this passage because it shows that *in this life, right now,* we are to reign with Christ. We have already been given all of His authority when we believed in Him, but we are not to wait until Heaven for this blessing. Christ's power within you allows you to take authority over the enemy, and live and reign in victory -- *right now! What are you waiting for?*

Journal:

Where have you neglected to take up your heavenly authority? Not to wield over others like a dictator, but to walk in victory, grace, and righteousness and show others the power of being united with Christ--*in this life*--not simply waiting for the next.

DECLARE:

I, _____, have received the gift of righteousness and reign as a king in life by Jesus Christ.

JOURNAL

DAY 34

Meditate on the Living Word...

▪ Ephesians 1:17-23

Reflect:

How beautiful to think of Paul praying for the church in this way. That we would grow in knowledge, wisdom, authority, understanding. Isn't that what we all want? To know the mysteries of God, to be enlightened of the things of God. In Christ, we are! And we can ask the Holy Spirit and Wisdom to grow in these areas as we spiritually mature. Keep asking! Keep seeking!

Journal:

▪ Where would you like to know more insights into the things of God? Some things God will keep a mystery, but much understanding and insight is given to those who ask. Do not be content to stay ignorant.

▪ Ask the Holy Spirit right now to guide you into further understanding. Dig into the Word and see where He will take you. Seek Wisdom herself, read about her in Proverbs 8. God loves to see His people desiring to grow and mature in their callings and God-given authority in Christ.

DECLARE:

I, _____, have received the spirit of wisdom and revelation in the knowledge of Jesus, the eyes of my understanding being enlightened.

JOURNAL

Meditate on the Living Word...
- Luke 6:37-38

Reflect:

Ah, to be free of judgement. A big lesson learned. What a freeing day it was for me when I let go of judging others, because I knew I didn't want to be judged in that way. I was being so hypocritical. What we give to others will be given to us. This goes back to love your neighbor as yourself. How do you want to be treated? Treat others accordingly. This applies to judgement, forgiveness, generosity. Let us be the examples abounding in love and grace, to point the way to Christ.

Journal:
- Where are you still being caught in judging others? Do you really want to be judged like that? God is the only righteous judge. It is His authority and responsibility, not ours.
- Repent and be set free from the chains of judgement.

DECLARE:

I, _____, have given, and it is given to me; good measure, pressed down, shaken together, and running over, men give into my bosom.

DAY 36

Meditate on the Living Word...

- Philippians 4:19-20

Reflect:

This can sometimes be a tough topic when we feel like we have legitimate physical needs that are not being met. Or when we get caught in comparison to others who seem to have more than us. But in Christ, we have no lack. How can those in poor villages still be happy and joyful when they have no material possessions? This life is not about accumulating wealth, it's about living in the spirit of abundance because we have *eternal* riches and glory awaiting us and in this life we have all we need in Christ.

Journal:

- Where may you be caught in the comparison trap?

- Or in entitlement thinking because you follow Christ? God did not promise us material wealth because we follow Him, but He says, "Seek ye first the Kingdom of God, and His righteousness. Then all these things will be added unto you."

- When our heart is set fully on seeking God and His Kingdom, our heart begins to change to gratitude and seeing the abundance already all around us. We no longer hunger and thirst for material things as our satisfaction and fulfillment. God is. Seek Him and repent of any wayward thinking you may have had.

DECLARE:

I, _____, have no lack for my God supplies all of my need according to His riches in glory by Christ Jesus.

JOURNAL

"Therefore, as God's chosen people, holy and dearly loved, clothe yourselves with compassion, kindness, humility, gentleness and patience."

COLOSSIANS 3:12

DAY 37

Meditate on the Living Word...

- Ephesians 6:10-18

Reflect:

Finally, we get to the powerful passage of the Armor of God. We need to put on our armor daily. The enemy is relentless against us, but God has given us all authority to overcome Him. *Hallelujah!* God has given us all the pieces we need for defense, and the powerful Sword of the Spirit, God's Word, as our offense. Use your offense daily by speaking out the truth of God's word over your life, health and circumstance. Do not grow idle!

Journal:

- Study each piece of the armor. What is the Holy Spirit revealing to you? Where is your armor lacking?
- Where does it need sharpening or tuning up? Where are you already very strong?
- Make a plan to grow stronger in each of these areas. How can you do that? Ask the Holy Spirit for guidance and action steps to direct your steps in fortifying your armor.

DECLARE:

I, _____, can quench all the fiery darts of the wicked one with my shield of faith.

JOURNAL

Meditate on the Living Word...

▪ Philippians 4:12-13

Reflect:

What do you think you are capable of?

What do you think God is capable of?

Are you limiting your potential and not taking action because you don't think you can do something in your own strength? You most likely cannot! And that's the point! We were created to have finite, limited capacity, but to marvel at a God who does not, and who chooses to work through His creation to accomplish great things.

Journal:

▪ What do you feel you want to do, or what God has put on your heart for you to do, but either you're exhausted trying to make it happen on your own, or you're frozen not doing anything because you feel too incapable and ill equipped?

▪ Write out those things and explore your limiting beliefs about yourself and about what God is capable of.

▪ Reflect and pray, asking God to remove your mental barriers and to give you the vision, strength and courage to take action.

DECLARE:

I, _____, can do all things through Christ Jesus.

JOURNAL

DAY 39

Meditate on the Living Word...
- 1 Peter 2:9-10

Reflect:

Wow. To be chosen by God. Individually. Purposefully. Just as you are. As He wants you to be. What blessing! What privilege! He has chosen us to become instruments of praise. Why do we praise Him? Because of who He is, what He's done for us, for humanity. Because He is the only one worthy and deserving of our unobstructed devotion, praise and honor. No one else is like Him. No person or other spiritual being. There is no one like our God.

Journal:
- Reflect on your love for God. What has He done in your life that deserves His praise? Where are you hesitant to praise and still struggling with distrust and hurt.
- Explore your feelings and do not hide them from God. He can handle any question or criticism, and desires to show you His goodness and mercy.

DECLARE:

I, _____, show forth the praises of God Who has called me out of darkness into His marvelous light.

JOURNAL

Meditate on the Living Word...

- 1 Peter 1:22-25
- Deuteronomy 14:1-2

Reflect:

To be born again of something imperishable, that will never end, eternal. Just think of it! This means enduring forever. As we have accepted God into our heart and allow His word to change us, we are stepping into a never-ending eternity, bathed in truth, righteousness and love. What hope we have, knowing the things of this earth will pass away, but we will be restored and reunited with God forever.

Journal:

- What do you think of when you think of something imperishable? What has been something perishable that has caused you hurt and pain?
- Take some time reflecting and praising God that His goodness, His righteousness, His love and mercy and character are imperishable. Never changing, never ending.

DECLARE:

I, _____, am God's child for I am born again of the incorruptible seed of the Word of God, which lives and abides forever.

Don't miss reading Mary's testimony on page 104...

JOURNAL

I was once a lonely isolated drug addict who was miserable full of fear worry and anxiety who hated life.

I am now by the grace of God a born again child of the Most High who has completely transformed me into a beautiful Believer who no longer is lonely isolated or full of fear.

Who has so many loving caring people in my life and I know without a shadow of a doubt how loved I am.

I never ever thought I'd be so forgiven and accepted but God has worked miracles in my life.

Be encouraged anytime and anywhere with our Healthy Christian Women podcast. Learn more at HealthyChristianWomen.com

"I can do all this through him who gives me strength."

PHILIPPIANS 4:13

Meditate on the Living Word...

- Ephesians 2:4-10

Reflect:

This is one of my most favorite verses in God's Word. It assures me that I was created on purpose, for a purpose. That God knew ahead of time, regardless of what would come my way, that He created me and knows every part of who I am. That I was created uniquely and intentionally to fulfill a special part in His grand design. What a gift you are to the world.

Journal:

- What do you think you were created to do or to be?
- Explore the times when you've not seen your uniqueness and your individuality as anything special and have not allowed your light to shine. What held you back and why?
- Now take a look at all the things that make you You. No one else has your exact combination of gifts, talents, passions and experiences, and no one else looks exactly like you either. You were hand-crafted, one-of-a-kind. How does that help you to see your purpose and marvel that your Heavenly Father deemed fit to make only one of you?

DECLARE:

I, _____, am God's workmanship, created in Christ unto good works.

JOURNAL

Meditate on the Living Word...

- 2 Corinthians 5:16-21

Reflect:

I love in verse 17 where we are reminded that we are a *new creation,* in the original Greek it translates to something unused, unworn, regenerated, unprecedented, novel. The idea that your new creation in Christ is completely separate from the old you. Never been seen before. The only one. Again God shows us how special, unique and on-purpose He has made us. You are so loved.

Journal:

- Reflect on the feeling when you get something brand new that you've never had. Or when you see something for the first time you've never seen. The awe. The wonder. The excitement. The possibilities. That is what God in your life did when you accepted Christ!
- Now it's time to start living in it, more than you ever have before. You are a new Creation!

DECLARE:

I, _____, am a new creature in Christ.

JOURNAL

DAY 43

Meditate on the Living Word...

Romans 6:8-14

1 Thessalonians 5:14-24

Reflect:

Have you ever wondered if you're a spirit having a human experience, or a human having a spiritual experience? It's the former. You were created before the foundations of the earth and God has chosen when it was the perfect time for your debut on earth. This human life is the only one we'll have. Cherish it, maximize it and use it wisely for the Lord.

Journal:

- When have you felt that you've wasted precious time? The resource that we can never get back. Praise God that one day we'll live with Him outside of the constraints of time. In *limitless* time.

- What are some time-sensitive things you want to accomplish with your remaining days on earth? Let any past regrets or wasted opportunities go. Take full advantage of what is still in front of you. If you're still here, on planet Earth, God has not called you home yet. You still have time on your hands. Use it to your best ability. Start creating a plan today.

DECLARE:

I, _____, am a spirit being alive to God.

JOURNAL

DAY 44

Meditate on the Living Word...

- 2 Corinthians 4:4-12

Reflect:

"This little light of mine, I'm gonna let it shine."

Have you ever been afraid to let your "light shine?" I know I have. But God has been building courage within me over the past few years, and it is still an evolving process. But God has given us so many blessings and miracles so that we will not keep them to ourselves, but that we would simply share them. Shed light on what He's done and who He is. Our world is full of darkness, but light pierces the dark and it cannot hide. You are that light.

Journal:

- When was a time you hid your light? What feelings were associated with that experience?
- When was a time you let your light shine? How did it feel?
- Ask God to continue to grow you and for opportunities to shine brightly to guide the way for others to find their true life in Christ.

DECLARE:

I, _____, am a Believer, and the light of the Gospel shines in my mind.

JOURNAL

DAY 45

Meditate on the Living Word...
- James 1:19-25

Reflect:

God calls us to be doers of His Word. To take action. Not to just read or listen to something that makes us feel good and to leave it there. We were created to be His vessels. To experience Him in and through us, serving and loving others. Let us not be superficial "Sunday Christians" but to truly allow God's truth to penetrate our hearts and minds, never leaving us the same.

Journal:

- Reflect on what stops you from being a "doer" 100%? Is it time? Energy? Opportunity? What has seemed to stop you in the past, and why is it important that you press on? We don't want to live in a place of "coulds" and "shoulds", lamenting on what could have been. Let the past be the past.

- But now God is calling you to put His word into action. He will bring the people and opportunities that need what you have to give. Step out in faith, ask God for courage and vision and begin seeing Him work all around you when you simply say, "Yes."

DECLARE:

I, _____, am a doer of the Word and blessed in my actions.

JOURNAL

"The Spirit himself testifies with our spirit that we are God's children. Now if we are children, then we are heirs—heirs of God and co-heirs with Christ, if indeed we share in his sufferings in order that we may also share in his glory."

ROMANS 8:16-17

Meditate on the Living Word...

▪ Romans 8:14-25

Reflect:

Being a joint-heir with Christ. Can you even imagine?! Think of the heirs to the wealthiest men in our current age. What splendor. What privilege. What vastly different lives from most of the world. Now imagine what awaits the heirs of God—the Creator of the Universe! *That is you and me!* As Paul says, all creation (including us) is in bondage, waiting to be liberated by Christ's triumphant return.

Journal:

▪ What comes to mind when you think of vastly wealthy heirs? Jealousy? Amazement? Excitement?

▪ Think of the glory that awaits *you* when you are liberated from this earthly body and the curse of sin and living in eternity in the splendor and majesty of God Himself.

▪ Take a moment to praise God for what awaits you in this life and in the next because of what Christ has done.

DECLARE:

I, _____, am a joint-heir with Christ.

JOURNAL

Meditate on the Living Word...

- Ephesians 1:3-10

Reflect:

To be adopted. That means to assume all rights and privileges of the one adopting you. To be fully chosen, intentionally, on purpose. Yes, God has only one begotten son, Jesus, but He has *chosen* each of us to assume the same rights and privileges, without repaying the price Jesus' paid! What Grace! What Love! Assume your rightful place of honor and privilege as God's own daughter.

Journal:

- When have you felt rejected? Unloved? Unlovable? Sadly it's a reality that far too many women have faced. But what does it feel like to be fully loved? Fully accepted? Fully chosen? It feels wonderful!

- Friend, God feels this way about YOU and wants you to start living like you believe it. What are some actions, thoughts and behaviors that would be different, if you were living from a place of fully believing who God says you are? Start taking action and living from that place. Cry out to God for what needs to be healed, released, forgiven and given grace so that it is no longer stopping you from living out of your true identity.

DECLARE:

I, _____, am His adopted daughter.

JOURNAL

DAY 48

Meditate on the Living Word...
- 2 Timothy 2:11-16

Reflect:

If others were to examine your life, would they find full integrity, no discrepancy between your public and private lives? If there is discrepancy, often times it's our striving to have others like, approve and accept us. But Beloved, you are fully approved by the Lord. Through Christ you have been made worthy of God's presence and love. You need no more striving. Let it go!

Journal:

- When have you tried to win the approval of others? What did it cost you? Was it worth it?

- What does it mean to you that your approval is made complete and whole in Christ to the Father. You do not need to strive to earn any more of His love, attention, favor or affection. He's given it ALL to you already, without holding back.

- Journal about what may be keeping you from accepting His gift of full approval, despite your imperfections.

DECLARE:

I, _____, am approved by God.

JOURNAL

Meditate on the Living Word...
- Acts 10:34-38

Reflect:

Acceptance seems to be an innate desire that we have. To be accepted by others, our parents, our peers. But sometimes our desire to be accepted is so strong it causes us to lose sight of who we truly are. We begin to compromise.

There is no need to try to earn your acceptance from God. You were chosen long before you were born, and you were created in His image. What higher sign of your acceptance and approval could there be?

Journal:
- When have you compromised yourself in order to gain acceptance from someone else?
- Humble yourself before the Lord and repent if needed. Praise Him that you don't need to put on any kind of "show" to win His favor. You already have it. Receive it. Walk in it. Share it.

DECLARE:

I, _____, am accepted just as I am.

Don't miss reading Jayme's testimony on page 126...

JOURNAL

JAYME'S STORY (DAY 49)

In one of Dr. Melody's programs, Heart-First Health, we began to explore our true identity in Christ. I realized I had so many Earthly identities placed on myself and that some of them were too hard to live up to or from my past that I didn't want to hold onto anymore.

When realizing where my true identity came from, in Christ, and all that comes with that, I really had an aha moment. It meant that I could have my identity be in Christ and it did not matter what other people identified me as or how I had identified myself.

That I only had to be who God saw me as.
Loved, cherished, special, unique, powerful, forgiven.

This has been so freeing and life-changing for me.

*Learn more about the Heart-First Health™ program Jayme mentions on page 187, or visit **bit.ly/heartfirsthealth***

"But whoever looks intently into the perfect law
that gives freedom, and continues in it—not
forgetting what they have heard, but doing it—
they will be blessed in what they do."

JAMES 1:25

DAY 50

Meditate on the Living Word...

- 2 Corinthians 5:18-21

Reflect:

Way back in the Garden, when sin entered our world, God already had a plan for His people's reconciliation. He does not want to spend any second longer away from you. He knew what had to be done. A spotless sacrifice would need to be made to a Holy God to make right what had gone wrong. And Jesus was obedient to do it. Obedient unto the cross for our reconciliation to glory.

Journal:

- Have you ever wanted something, but the price was too high—you could not buy it? Think on what that was and how you felt when you couldn't have it.

- Have you ever wanted to be with someone, but they did not want you back? The pain that that caused your heart. God's heart breaks when His people do not choose Him back, even though Jesus paved the way for all to receive Him. Jesus paid the price we could never pay.

- Reflect and praise God that you have said yes to Him and praise Jesus for the price He paid for your reconciliation back to your Abba Father.

DECLARE:

Through Jesus I, _____, am reconciled back to God.

JOURNAL

DAY 51

Meditate on the Living Word...
- Deuteronomy 32:10-12

Reflect:

Do you ever get uncomfortable being the center of attention? Well, you will always be the center of God's attention. He can't help it. He's utterly captivated by *you*. But we often feel uncomfortable with that much attention, and we *know* we're not deserving or worthy of that level of adoration. We wonder, *"What is God thinking? I'm far from perfect. How can I be truly loved just as I am?"* But He sees deeper. He sees His masterpiece. What's not to love?

Journal:

- Have there ever been times that someone's attention toward you was uncomfortable or inappropriate? Sadly many have been victims of unwanted attention, and this comes in many forms. Continue to seek healing if that has been the case for you.

- Ask God to help you see that His love for you is and will never be inappropriate or manipulated. His love is far above any human love. He loves your soul because He created you, and He never creates anything on accident or that is not perfect in His sight.

DECLARE:

I, _____, am the apple of His eye.

JOURNAL

DAY 52

Meditate on the Living Word...

- Colossians 3:1-10

Reflect:

When Paul refers to being *"hidden in Christ"*, the Greek meaning is not necessarily to hide and conceal, but, *"to be kept laid up in Heaven."* No longer on this earth. Waiting in glory. What a powerful understanding of this verse! That when we accepted Christ and our old self died, we are then taken away and "laid up in Heaven" with Him, in our rightful home. But we are to return with Christ when He returns.

What has been laid up, out of earthly sight, will be made visible again with Christ's return, where we will reign with him on the new earth. *Hallelujah!*

Journal:

Spend some time journaling praises to God for all the things He's saved you from when you gave your life to Him, and all that awaits you in glory. Reigning with Christ in glory. What an incredible notion to behold.

DECLARE:

I, _____, am hidden in Christ.

Meditate on the Living Word...
- Galatians 5:13-18

Reflect:

Powerful verses as Paul sums up the entire law: To be free from sin, and to love our neighbor as ourselves. We are selfish people. We do just about anything in service to ourselves. But how much and what do we do for *others*? Everyone else is our neighbor. If we are so generous to ourselves and our own self-seeking nature, why are we not the same to everyone else? This is the kind of love, passion and concern we are called to have and that God wants to see His people display.

Journal:
- Reflect on a time where you did something really nice to pamper yourself. How did it feel?
- Do you think someone else would also like to enjoy that kind of experience?
- Ask God to show you how you can be more generous to others and even the scales of what you do for yourself and for others.

DECLARE:

I, _____, love my neighbor as myself.

JOURNAL

DAY 54

Meditate on the Living Word...

■ Romans 8:26-30

Reflect:

Have you answered the call? The invitation extended to you by God himself to receive eternal salvation? Take hold of it, with all its rights and privileges. *It is yours!* But it's not just to wait until glory to enjoy it. Jesus told us His kingdom is here-*now*. Let us step into His glory by engaging with Him in our earthly lives and allowing Him to work in and through us and to bring more souls into eternity with Him. Let's take hold of it today!

Journal:

■ Journal praise to God for his invitation into glory with Him and that you said yes. Ask Him to show you ways you can interact with His unseen world while you're still living on this side of Heaven.

■ Write a prayer right now for someone you know who does not yet know the Lord and has not yet accepted their invitation for salvation. Ask the Lord to open doors and to give you the words to share about who He is and what He's done in your life, and for boldness to ask them if they want to know Jesus personally as well.

DECLARE:

I, _____, am called and destined for eternal salvation.

JOURNAL

"For we are His workmanship, created in Christ Jesus for good works, which God prepared beforehand so that we would walk in them."

EPHESIANS 2:10

Meditate on the Living Word...
- Ephesians 1:11-14

Reflect:

I love the idea of the Holy Spirit being a deposit on what is to come in Heaven. God truly has given us everything when He said His kingdom is at hand, already here once Jesus came on the scene. The fact that we have the Holy Spirit inside of us to not only be our Guide, Comforter and Truth, but He has been given to us as a deposit and seal. To allow us to experience a little taste of Heaven in our daily lives until we are fully called Home. This is why we must never grieve the Holy Spirit. We do not want to reject and squander our deposit from Heaven.

Journal:
- Have you ever grieved the Holy Spirit? Known He wanted you to do something, but you did not.
- Take some time to properly repent and grieve over your actions, as well as to release your past to the Lord. He forgives us fully, as soon as we ask with a contrite spirit. Praise Him for His goodness, mercy and righteousness.

DECLARE:

I, _____, am sealed with the Holy Spirit.

Meditate on the Living Word...

- Matthew 5:13

Reflect:

It's true that if salt became unsalty, it would no longer serve its purpose and be useful they way it was meant to be. Jesus is warning us that our purpose is to be useful in sharing the gospel. This is why we were created. And as we have come to know God, we are to lead others to Him as well. God's desire is that all of His children would desire a relationship with Him and to have their name written in the Book of Life. Let's not lose our usefulness. God can use us anywhere and in any way. *Are we willing?*

Journal:

- Think back and reflect on the ways you've seen God use you. How you've been able to be a blessing to someone else, even in the smallest way. That's your proverbial saltiness. Your usefulness. God was working through you to meet the needs of another one of His Beloved's.

- Ask Him to reveal to you how else He has created you with the purpose to be helpful and useful to those around you, right where you are. Allow the Holy Spirit to give you fresh ideas and revelation and to show you new creative ways you can put yourself to use for God's glory. *"Bloom where you are planted."*

DECLARE:

I, _____, am the salt of the earth.

JOURNAL

Meditate on the Living Word...

- 1 John 5:1-12

Reflect:

Because of Jesus we not only overcome the world and it's sin, but we overcome death through eternal life in Christ. The life we not live is only the precursor of our eternal life that we will one day step into. How incredible is that?

Do not wait for Heaven before you begin enjoying life. Celebrate all Jesus has done and overcome on your behalf, so that in this life you may life free! Free from sin, from doubt, from shame, from death. *Give Him praise today!*

Journal:

- Write about all the things you can think of that Jesus has overcome so that you no longer have to be bound by sin and it's mess. What are some snares and traps you continually find yourself falling into?

- Ask God for His way out and His strength and peace to do it. You were not meant to live in bondage any longer. Sin has no more hold on you. *Amen!!*

DECLARE:

I, _____, am an overcomer.

JOURNAL

Meditate on the Living Word...
- Revelation 1:4-8

Reflect:

We owe everything to Jesus. Because of Him we are able to be in the presence of God. Because of Him we are redeemed and washed clean by His blood. Because of Him we are made holy and made co-heirs with Christ in Heaven. What privilege, what blessing, what honor. Thank you, Jesus.

Journal:

- Pour out your praise to God for what He has done for us, and to Jesus for His sacrifice that we may be made a joint-heir with Him for eternity.
- Allow the awe and wonder of that to wash over you, resulting in praise and thanksgiving to God.

DECLARE:

I, _____, am a king and a priest of the Most High.

JOURNAL

"And we know that in all things God works for the good of those who love Him, who have been called according to his purpose."

ROMANS 8:28

Meditate on the Living Word...
- John 15:9-17

Reflect:

Friends share things with one another. Their thoughts, their possessions, their time, their love. Being a friend is an honor and a very special place to hold in someone's life. And Jesus says we are His friends—that He does not keep secrets, but shares with us the voice of the Father so that we too may walk in the knowledge of God. What a blessing to be a friend of God himself.

Journal:

- Think of a great friend you've had. The blessing of that friendship. The laughter, the tears, the breaking of bread together. There's something very special about good friendship. It nourishes the soul.

- As you think of Jesus, God himself, as your friend, recount how He has demonstrated His friendship to you.

- What experiences have you had together, that only you two share? What kind of a friend are you to God? Are you upholding the qualities of a good friend?

- Where can you grow in your relationship with God and be a good friend right back to God?

DECLARE:

I, _____, am a friend of God.

JOURNAL

DAY 60

Meditate on the Living Word...

- Psalm 127:1-2

Reflect:

These two powerful verses cut right to the heart. Where are we laboring and toiling in vain? On our own pursuits, ambitions and plans, versus sitting at the Lord's feet, awaiting His instruction and taking action as He leads? Do we reject the easy yolk, the light burden, the rest? He gives rest to His beloved. Do you rest? Or do you toil away in busyness and self-sufficient pride...

Journal:

- Reflect on times you've made your own busyness, your own work that was not instructed or directed by God. Did it work out? Did you get everything you were striving for? You are His beloved, and to his beloved He grants rest. He does not make you labor and toil needlessly.

- Are you willing to receive His rest? To wait at His feet and go when He says go, stop when He says stop? Or are you evading the rest your soul so desperately desires?

DECLARE:

I, _____, am his beloved.

JOURNAL

Meditate on the Living Word...

- Psalm 112:1-10

Reflect:

The blessings of the Lord abound!! This entire psalm proclaims the blessings of being one of God's chosen and the destruction of those who do not honor God. You, my Dear, are blessed!

If you ever find yourself down, overwhelmed or anxious, take a moment to start counting your blessings. In no time you will realize your momentary troubles are but a blip compared to you abundant blessings and eternity in Heaven waiting for you.

Journal:

- Begin taking an accounting of your blessings.
- Start by writing all the major categories of your life across the top of a page: Work, Family, Community, Possessions, Health etc.Then under each main category begin writing everything and everyone you can think of that applies.
- You will be amazed. By the time you're done you will have a tangible piece of evidence of just how blessed you truly are. We take so much for granted, don't we?

DECLARE:

I, _____, am blessed.

JOURNAL

Meditate on the Living Word...

- Hebrews 12:1-3

Reflect:

Jesus asked that his cup be taken from him. To not endure the cross. But he relinquished, "Not my will, but thine be done." And willingly, obediently went to the cross. What prize could have been so great that He would endure so much? You. Me. *Us.*

Full reconciliation with the Father available to all. We were the joy set before Him. He saw our lives, our purpose, our path and knew we would not want to miss out on the glory and splendor of eternity with Him. He did what only He could do to atone for our sins. We are the joy set before Him.

Journal:

- Think of the sacrifice Jesus made for you. Allow the fullness of the weight of it be made known in your heart.

- The fact that you are so precious to God that He would pay the price for the entire world so we could be made worthy and holy of a personal relationship with him, only through Christ, is an overwhelming thought. But it's the *truth.*

- Write your love, adoration, praise and exaltation to God in response to what Jesus did for you on the cross that day.

- You will see Him face-to-face one day and reign with Him in glory. He didn't want to have eternal life without you. What love!

DECLARE:

I, _____, am the joy set before him.

JOURNAL

"As the Father has loved me, so have I loved you.
Now remain in my love."

JOHN 15:9

Meditate on the Living Word...
- 2 Corinthians 1:20-22

Reflect:

We say "amen" so often, sometimes we don't understand what it really means. It signifies agreement, "so be it, so it is, may it be fulfilled."

Paul is reminding us here that in Christ all of God's promises are "Yes and Amen." Jesus not only died for our sins but He fulfilled all prophecy and law and completed God's atonement work for the world. In Christ we live and move and have our being. It is through Him we have access and become privy to receiving God's promises. *What blessing!*

Journal:

- Explore what promises you don't think you're worthy of. Repent as the Holy Spirit leads. Come before the Lord praising Him for His forgiveness and grace and confessing that through His son Jesus you have been granted all rights and privileges with Christ. *Step into your blessings!*
- Take a moment to literally count your blessings.

DECLARE:

I, _____, am anointed.

JOURNAL

DAY 64

Meditate on the Living Word...

- Genesis 1:26-27

Reflect:

We are made in the image of God. What does that really mean? It means God has imparted qualities of himself to us, but it also means we are not God. We were made to be similar but that we are to recognize our limits compared to His limitlessness. We have been blessed to create, to imagine, to bring forth, to birth, to speak, to have power--but we are to always recognize these qualities are but a shadow of the immenseness of our Creator.

Journal:

- Journal about a time where you began to have a "God-complex." Where you thought you were the be-all-end-all and the highest and best above others. The Ultimate power. Ask the Holy Spirit to reveal the deep roots of pride that contribute to thinking and acting in this way.
- We remember that Jesus tells us the least will be the greatest, and the greatest will be least in His Kingdom.
- Repent where necessary from the sins of pride, and willfully humble yourself as you see the shadow that you are compared to the Almighty God. Praise Him that there is only One like Him.

DECLARE:

I, _____, am made in the image of God.

JOURNAL

Meditate on the Living Word...

- Job 10:8-12

Reflect:

God does not make mistakes, and everything He creates He deems "good." The term good is so much more than we typically think of it. It means pleasant, pleasing, excellent, happy, prosperous. That's what God did when He created you. He deemed when it was time for your grand entrance to Earth and created you on purpose and for a purpose. You, my Dear, are exquisitely fashioned by your Creator.

Journal:

- Journal about something that you would describe as exquisitely fashioned. Is it an object, a place, a person? What feelings and thoughts does it illicit? Now turn that on yourself. Every good thing you associate with that, is what God associates with You!

- Spend some time allowing that kind of love to wash over you and praise Him for His goodness.

DECLARE:

I, _____, am exquisitely fashioned.

JOURNAL

Meditate on the Living Word...

- 1 Peter 2:1-9

Reflect:

What a powerful analogy. A stone. Jesus the Cornerstone, and us the additional stones. Firm, solid, secure, powerful, mighty, substantial-- with life and breath!

And the other good news is that all of those powerful qualities are not on our shoulders to bear. They are because of our Chief Cornerstone, Jesus. It is through Him and His power that we become living stones.

Journal:

- Reflect on a time where you felt you had the world on your shoulders. Where it was "all up to you." It's super overwhelming, right? We weren't supposed to carry that much stress and weight around. We weren't built for it. But you know who was? Jesus.

- Take this time to cast your burdens onto Him.

- He can take them and He can give you the strength you need to be that solid rock, that stone. But without Him you will fail and be crushed under the weight of life's pressures.

- Declare who your true strength comes from and let go in faith that He will strengthen, guide and uphold you.

- He was designed to do it. We were designed to let Him.

DECLARE:

I, _____, am a living stone.

JOURNAL

"Therefore, since we are surrounded by such a great cloud of witnesses, let us throw off everything that hinders and the sin that so easily entangles. And let us run with perseverance the race marked out for us..."

HEBREWS 12:1

Meditate on the Living Word...
- John 15:1-11

Reflect:

I love these verses and analogy of the vine and it's branches. It makes the visual easy to understand and it makes our role and duty easy to take action. We allow God to do his pruning, He sees the whole plant and knows what's best and for our good. We remain connected to Him, intentionally abiding and gaining spiritual nourishment.

And what is the reward? The result? That our joy may be made complete by the Lord. He wants to give you joy as a fruit of the Spirit. But we must remain connected in order to benefit and experience the beautiful fruit basket of rewards and blessings.

Journal:

- What does your spiritual "fruit basket" look like?
- What fruits to you want to have more of?
- What fruits are absent or withering and not being properly fed or nourished?
- Where is God prompting you to take more action in your abiding with Him in order to produce more fruit?

DECLARE:

I, _____, am a branch.

JOURNAL

Meditate on the Living Word...

- John 8:28-32

Reflect:

To be one's disciple is to adhere to their teachings, to follow and to replicate. Jesus is saying we are all His disciples who believe what He says and follow Him. He promises we will know the truth and the truth shall set us free. Isn't that what we're really after? In a world full of lies, deception and false doctrine, our hearts are longing to have the real truth that will dispel and overcome the lies.

Trust in His word, Sweet One. It is unshakeable and your life will change as you begin living and acting as though you really believe it. Take that leap of faith.

Journal:

- How have Jesus' teachings, life and example led you into truth? How have you been set free by God's truth?

- Ask God to show you more areas where you faith is waning and needs to be transformed by His truth. Seek Him for healing and deliverance and step into freedom once-and-for-all.

- Declare who your true strength comes from and let go in faith that He will strengthen, guide and uphold you.

- He was designed to do it. We were designed to let Him.

DECLARE:

I, _____, am His disciple.

JOURNAL

Meditate on the Living Word...

- Romans 12:3-8

Reflect:

We are an incredible creation. We are a human body with a living soul, connected with the Spirit of God living inside of us. What we cannot do!

Your unique gifts, talents, passions, experiences and abilities make you uniquely qualified to be the hands and feet of Jesus to everyone around you, right where you are. Ponder the wonder and majesty of this.

Journal:

- If you were God, living inside of a human being you created, chosen to be your representative, what would you want them to do? To say? To act?

- From that perspective, how do you feel you've been doing as God's chosen temple and body to interact with the world? Where do you need to change, grow, or learn to be more submissive or obedient?

- Marvel at the wonder that God Almighty has chosen to work through you in this way. And when you said Yes to Him, you said No to yourself. You are not your own. You are a dutiful servant and steward of the life He's given you.

DECLARE:

I, _____, am his body.

JOURNAL

Meditate on the Living Word...
- Isaiah 40:27-31

Reflect:
Look at all of the verbs in this passage describing what happens to those who hope in the Lord: increase, run, walk, soar, renew. At some point you will come to the end of your own understanding and own strength. This is when we need the Lord more than ever! We must keep our hope in Him alive and well through every season of life, so that when the trials come, our hope is strong and we will see God's promises coming to life right in front of our eyes.

Journal:
- Think back on a time where your strength ran out. Where you had no choice but to depend on the Lord. What did He do? How did He bring you through? Did your faith falter or thrive?
- Declare to the Lord today that you will not let yourself get to the point of exhaustion before you finally lean on Him. Allow Him to give you strength long before you need it. Allow it to be a continual supply from Him, not your own.

DECLARE:

I, _____, am strong in Him.

JOURNAL

"...you also, as living stones, are being built up--
a spiritual house, a holy priesthood, to offer up
spiritual sacrifices acceptable to God through
Jesus Christ."

1 PETER 2:5

Meditate on the Living Word...
- Colossians 3:5-11

Reflect:

We are called to live differently once we've been saved. Not only called, but for many, there is an intrinsic change that no longer wants to go back. Let us check our hearts if we are still giving into our "old" man, before we were saved: anger, rage, malice, slander, and filthy language. We should have none of them, and want none of them. Rise above and put on your new righteousness in Christ.

Journal:

- Where have you found yourself still living in the ways of your "old" man. Pre-saved You. If you're struggling, these are areas that God is revealing where you need deeper healing. Healing from old wounds, forgiveness, peace.

- Seek professional counseling and services to guide you when you cannot do it on your own. God has equipped many to help in these areas.

- Do not "settle", with a victim mindset thinking you can't, or don't need to change. Pursue further healing until you are truly free.

DECLARE:

I, _____, have put off the old man and have put on the new man, which is renewed in the knowledge after the image of Him Who created me.

JOURNAL

DAY 72

Meditate on the Living Word...

- Mark 16:15-18
- Luke 10:17-20

Reflect:

What power! What protection! Do you truly believe Jesus at His word? Miracles in Jesus' name happen daily. Do not have a hardened heart thinking they were only for "olden days." Jesus is alive, His name is true, and His power is still working in the earth. Don't believe me? Do a Google or YouTube search and you will see.

Journal:

What miracles have you witnessed or heard about in Jesus' name? Have you ever done any yourself? Jesus' power is within you. Give it life! It is how others will come to know Him. Do not keep it hidden.

DECLARE:

I, _____, have received the power of the Holy Spirit to lay hands on the sick and see them recover, to cast out demons, to speak with new tongues. I have power over all the power of the enemy, and nothing shall by any means harm me.

Your Full Identity in Christ with all 72 unique attributes follows in the next section. Don't miss this powerful life-declaration of who you are in Christ.

JOURNAL

Your Full Identity in Christ Declaration

- READ ALOUD AND WITH POWER -

"I, _____, am . . .

More than a conqueror, an overcomer, a partaker of His divine nature, an ambassador for Christ, a chosen generation, a royal priesthood, a holy nation, a purchased people, the righteousness of God in Jesus Christ, a temple of the Holy Spirit, the head and not the tail, above only and not beneath, the light of the world, His elect, full of mercy, kindness, humility and long suffering, forgiven of all my sins and washed in the blood, delivered from the power of darkness and translated into God's Kingdom, redeemed and overflowing the gratitude, called to be the voice of His praise, healed by the stripes of Jesus, raised up, greatly loved, strengthened, submitted. The devil flees from me because I resist him in the name of Jesus. I press on, I do not have a spirit of fear, but of power, love and a sound mind. I have been crucified with Christ. I am complete, alive, free from the law of sin and death. I am far from oppression, born of God and the evil one does not touch me. I am holy and without blame before Him in love,

I have the mind of Christ and the peace of God that passes all understanding. I have received the gift of righteousness and reign as a king in life by Jesus Christ. I have received the spirit of wisdom and revelation in the knowledge of Jesus, the eyes of my understanding being enlightened. I have received the power of the Holy Spirit to lay hands on the sick and see them recover, to cast out demons to speak with new tongues.

I have power over the enemy and nothing shall by any means harm me. I have put on the new man, which is renewed in the knowledge of God. I have given and it has been given to me: good measure, pressed down, shaken together, and running over. I have no lack for God supplies all of my needs according to His riches in glory by Christ Jesus. I quench all the fiery darts of the wicked one with my shield of faith.

I can do all things through Christ Jesus. I show forth the praises of God who has called me out of darkness into His marvelous light. I am God's child for I am born again of the incorruptible seed of the word of God. I am God's workmanship. I am a new creature, a spirit being alive to God, a believer, the light of the Gospel shines in my mind, a doer of the word and blessed my actions. I am a joint-heir with Christ, the apple of His eye, hidden in Christ.

I am called, destined, sealed; the salt of the earth. I am an overcomer, a king and priest of the Most High. A friend of God, His beloved. I am blessed, the joy set before him, anointed, made in the image of God, exquisitely fashioned, a living Stone, a branch, a disciple, His body, and I am strong in Him."

What Comes Next?

Have you enjoyed your journey? No doubt God has been doing powerful things in your heart thus far. You are now ready to take the next step!

Introducing: **Heart-First Health™**

Inspired and led by the Holy Spirit, I've created this biblically-based program to take you through an 8-week journey of experiencing greater heart and mind healing and growth in the Lord. Get ready to ignite deeper passion and purpose at any age or stage of your life.

Your Identity in Christ is just the beginning.

Join me, Dr. Melody, on this life-changing journey into true freedom, health and wholeness in Christ.

https://bit.ly/heartfirsthealth

Index

About The Author

Dr. Melody Stevens is a Doctor of Physical Therapy and Certified Health Coach. After opening her private practice in the summer of 2012, God began to move in her heart that she could no longer just treat her patient's physical symptoms and ailments. He gave her a powerful message and passion that she could not keep inside. Our health is not just made up of our physical body—our appearance, our size, our physical condition.

True health, as He created it to be, comes from the beautiful dance of our mental, physical and spiritual wellbeing, all working together. Each element affecting and playing off one another in powerfully interconnected ways.

Fueled by this message, Fit+Faith was born in August of 2015.

Since that time, the Fit+Faith community of Christian women has grown worldwide, strengthened by the Healthy Christian Women podcast that debuted in January of 2018.

Dr. Melody loves to speak and empower women at conferences, events, retreats and workshops. She has developed numerous programs, resources, trainings, and online micro-communities all with the express purpose of nurturing your mental, physical and/or spiritual health. This is what we call our *Trilogy of Health*, or *Health Trilogy.*

The Rooted In Christ Devotional & Journal that you hold in your hands was developed to nurture your spiritual health of your Health Trilogy. One of the key strongholds that Dr. Melody has seen in Christian women today are lies of unworthiness, fear and shame.

Fortunately, each of these vices are completely broken with the truth of God's Word, the power of our identity in Christ and the word of our testimony. *Amen!*

Dive in and join our global community of Christian women at Fit+Faith. Learn more at **www.fitplusfaith.com.**